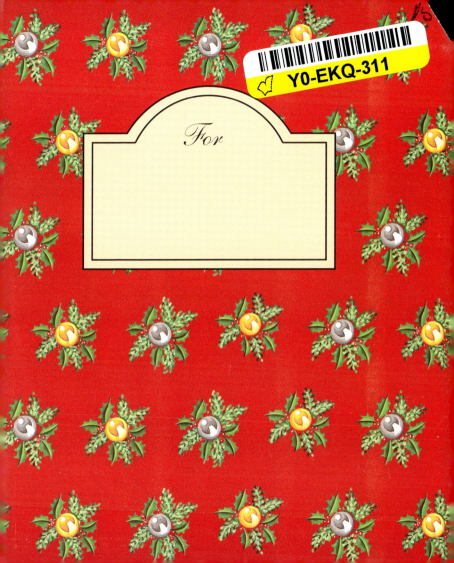

For

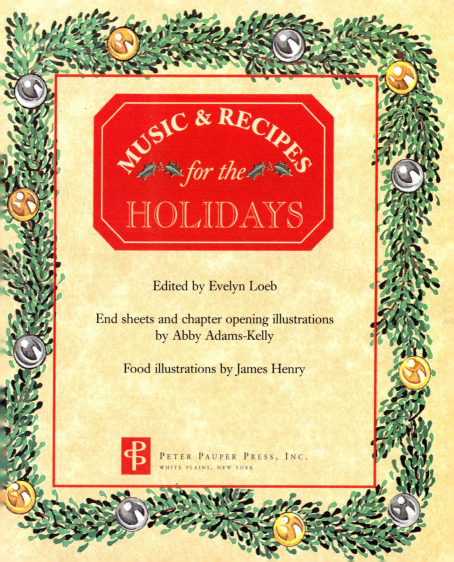

MUSIC & RECIPES
for the
HOLIDAYS

Edited by Evelyn Loeb

End sheets and chapter opening illustrations
by Abby Adams-Kelly

Food illustrations by James Henry

PETER PAUPER PRESS, INC.
WHITE PLAINS, NEW YORK

To Ethel Mills, for her help in testing many of the
recipes herein, and for her friendship.

Original book design by Deborah Michel. Revised design
for this edition by Arlene Greco.

Copyright © 1997
Peter Pauper Press, Inc.
202 Mamaroneck Avenue
White Plains, NY 10601
All rights reserved
ISBN 0-88088-892-X
Printed in Singapore
7 6 5 4 3 2 1

CONTENTS

INTRODUCTION

What is the most memorable part of a joyous Christmas celebration? Good food, shared with people you love, of course!

*M*usic and Recipes for the Holidays *will help you decide on a menu for your feast, and its time-tested recipes will assure your success. These are traditional dishes, meant to provide delicious memories for all who partake of them. And playing the enclosed CD while you cook will be sure to put you in a Holiday mood.*

So gather family and friends, and have a wonderful Holiday dinner. Merry Christmas!

THE EDITOR

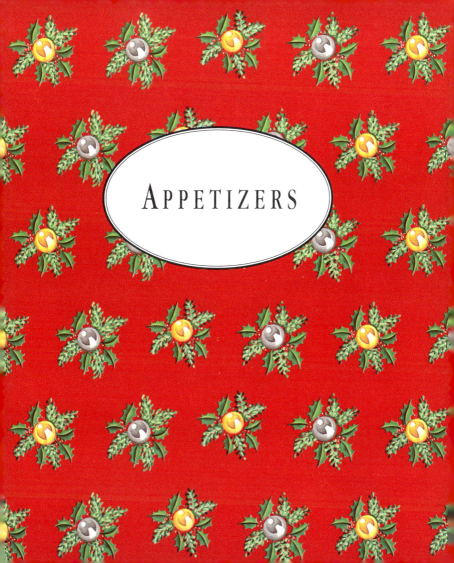

APPETIZERS

OYSTERS ROCKEFELLER

36 oysters on the half shell
Rock salt
2 cups cooked and drained spinach
1/4 cup chopped scallions
2 tablespoons minced parsley
2 tablespoons finely chopped celery
1/2 teaspoon salt
6 drops hot pepper sauce
1/3 cup butter
2 teaspoons anisette
1/2 cup fine dry bread crumbs

Put oysters in their shells on a bed of rock salt so they will remain upright and not lose their juice. Combine spinach, scallions, parsley, and celery. Put this mixture through a food grinder. Add salt and hot pepper sauce, mixing well.

Cook mixture in butter and anisette over low heat for 4 or 5 minutes. Fold in bread crumbs and spread 1

tablespoon of mixture on each oyster. Bake in a 400°
oven for 10 minutes or until lightly browned.

GUACAMOLE

2 avocados
1 tomato, chopped
1/2 onion, minced
1 tablespoon lime or lemon juice
1/4 teaspoon garlic salt
Salt and pepper

If avocados are hard when you buy them, allow to ripen (not in the refrigerator!) until they begin to feel a little bit soft to the touch. Peel, cut in half, remove stones, and mash avocado with other ingredients. Use as party dip with corn chips or tortilla chips, or use as garnish on any salad. Dabs of guacamole may be topped with a teaspoon of sour cream sprinkled with paprika for added decoration.

STUFFED CRAB

8 oz. pasteurized lump backfin crab meat, drained
*   and picked over*
1/2 cup cornbread stuffing mix (optional)
1/3 cup butter, divided
1 cup half and half
2 tablespoons flour
3 shallots, diced
2 tablespoons madeira or sherry
1/4 teaspoon anchovy paste
Grated peel of 1/2 lemon
Chopped fresh parsley for garnish

In 2 tablespoons butter sauté shallots until wilted; add stuffing and sauté until slightly browned. Mix with crabmeat and set aside. Sauté flour in remaining butter; add half and half to make thin bechamel. Add madeira, and cook until alcohol is burned off. Add anchovy paste and lemon peel. Allow to thicken. Toss with crab and stuffing mixture. Add parsley. Bake 20 to 25 minutes at 350°. Serve with crackers.

11

SPINACH DIP

1 package frozen chopped spinach, thawed and
  drained well
1 envelope vegetable soup mix
1 can sliced water chestnuts, finely chopped
1/3 cup finely sliced green onions
1 pint sour cream
1 cup mayonnaise
Freshly ground black pepper to taste
1 round loaf of bread

Mix ingredients except bread and chill well. Cut off the
top of the loaf of bread and reserve it. Carefully cut
around the edge of the bread about 1" in from the edge.
Remove the bread in the center and cut it into bite-size
pieces. Do the same with the reserved bread top. Put the
well-chilled dip into the center of the hollowed-out bread
and arrange the pieces of the cut-up bread on the edge of
the plate around the filled loaf and serve.

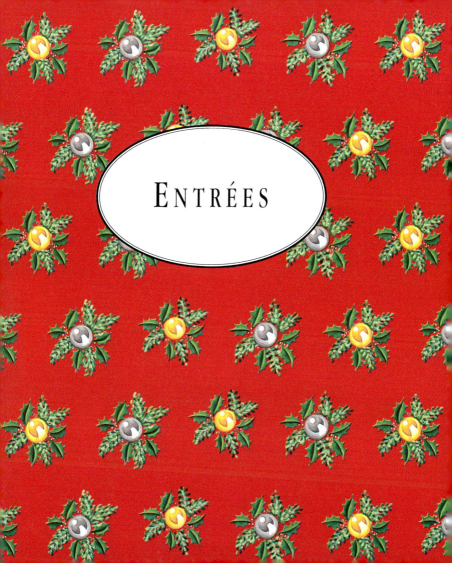

ENTRÉES

STANDING RIB ROAST

Select a 2- or 3-rib standing rib roast (4 to 5 pounds).
Place fat side up in roasting pan; season with salt and
pepper and place in 350° oven. Do not cover and do not
add water.

Allow 18 to 20 minutes per pound for rare roast,
22 to 25 minutes per pound for medium, and 27 to 30
minutes per pound for well-done. Serve with Yorkshire
Pudding.

YORKSHIRE PUDDING

1/2 cup drippings from rib roast

5 eggs

2 cups milk

2 cups flour

1/4 teaspoon salt

Pour drippings from rib roast into approximately 10" x 12" pan. Preheat pan with fat in oven. Beat remaining ingredients until evenly blended, but do not overbeat. Pour mixture into pan and bake at 450° about 30 minutes.

ROAST TURKEY

Dress and clean turkey. Rub inside with salt and pepper. Stuff neck cavity. Fasten opening with metal pins. Fill body cavity loosely with stuffing. Rub with butter or make paste of 1/2 cup butter, 3/4 cup flour; spread over all parts of turkey.

Place turkey breast side down in open roasting pan to allow juices to run down into breast. Drip pan from broiler may be used if large roaster is not available. Roast uncovered in 300-325° oven 15 to 20 minutes per pound, turning turkey over onto back when half done.

Baste at 30-minute intervals with mixture of melted butter and hot water. When breast and legs become light brown, cover with brown paper. Turkey is done when meat pulls away from leg bones.

ROAST GOOSE

Preheat oven to 450°. Wash goose in cold water and wipe dry. Sprinkle with salt and pepper. Stuff with bread stuffing. Place breast side up on rack in roasting pan. Prick all over with fork. Pour 2 cups boiling water over goose and reduce oven to 350°. Roast 25 to 30 minutes per pound. For stuffed goose, add another 20 minutes to cooking time. When goose is done, garnish with cranberries and watercress, and serve with apple sauce.

CHESTNUT STUFFING

1 cup butter

1 cup minced onion

1 teaspoon thyme

1 teaspoon sage

1-1/2 teaspoons salt

3/4 teaspoon pepper

1/3 cup chopped parsley

3/4 cup chopped celery and leaves

8 cups soft stale bread crumbs or cubes

1 pound Italian chestnuts, cooked, shelled and chopped

Melt butter in skillet and add all ingredients except bread crumbs and chestnuts. Cook 5 minutes. Add crumbs and chestnuts. Makes about 10 cups of turkey stuffing.

PRUNE STUFFING

10 cups fine dry bread crumbs

3/4 cup chopped onion

2-1/2 cups peeled, cored, coarsely chopped tart
   apples

1/4 teaspoon salt

2 teaspoons poultry seasoning

3/4 pound prunes, pitted and cut into small pieces

6 tablespoons melted butter

Mix all ingredients well.

BREAD CRUMB STUFFING

4 cups dry bread crumbs
1 medium onion, chopped
1 teaspoon salt
1/4 teaspoon pepper
Sage to taste
Parsley, chopped
1/4 teaspoon poultry seasoning
1/3 cup melted butter
Hot water or stock to moisten

Combine bread crumbs, onion, and seasonings; add butter and sufficient liquid to moisten. Mix gently. Allow 1 cup stuffing for each pound of poultry or game.

BAKED VIRGINIA HAM

Place ham fat side up on rack in open roasting pan. Add 1/3 inch of water to pan. Do not cover. Bake in 350° oven, allowing 20 minutes per pound for a large ham, 25 minutes per pound for a small ham, and 30 minutes per pound for a half ham. Roast meat thermometer registers 170° when ham is done. Ham may be basted during cooking period with ginger ale or cider. For the last half hour of baking, rub surface with mustard and brown sugar. Score fat in diamonds; stick a whole clove in each.

Stuffed Crown Roast of Lamb

1/2 cup chopped celery
1 medium onion, chopped
2 cloves garlic, minced
3 tablespoons salad oil
4 cups soft bread crumbs or cubes
2 tablespoons chopped parsley
1/2 teaspoon rosemary
Salt and pepper
1 16-rib crown roast of lamb
6 strips bacon
Raw potato
Flour
Currant jelly

Preheat oven to 325°. Sauté celery, onion, and garlic in oil until almost tender. Add bread crumbs or cubes, parsley, rosemary, 1 teaspoon salt, and pepper to taste; blend thoroughly. Sprinkle roast with salt and pepper and fill with bread crumb mixture. Stand on a rack in a roasting pan. Nick sides of bacon strips and place over stuffing. Place pieces of potato on tips of ribs to keep them from charring. Place in oven and roast about 30 minutes per pound. Place roast on platter and remove bacon and potato. Keep warm while preparing gravy. Thicken pan drippings with a little flour; season to taste with currant jelly. Place paper frills on ribs and serve with gravy. 8 servings of two ribs each.

BOILED LOBSTERS

2 live lobsters (1 pound each)
3 quarts boiling water
3 tablespoons salt
Melted butter

Plunge lobsters headfirst into boiling salted water. Cover and return to boiling point. Simmer for 20 minutes. Drain. Place lobster on its back. With a sharp knife cut in half lengthwise. Remove stomach, which is just back of head, and intestinal vein, which runs from stomach to tip of tail. Do not discard green liver and coral roe; they are delicious. Crack claws. Serve with melted butter.

BROILED SALMON STEAKS

8 salmon steaks
Juice of 1 lemon
Flour for dredging
Salad oil
Salt
Paprika

Sprinkle salmon steaks generously with lemon juice. Flour one side only. Place floured side down in preheated broiler pan containing enough oil to cover bottom of pan. Turn immediately. Sprinkle with salt and paprika and broil until well browned without further turning, or about 10 minutes per inch of thickness. 8 servings.

SALMON SAUCE

4 egg yolks

1 cup olive oil

2 tablespoons vinegar

3 teaspoons French mustard

2 teaspoons English mustard

1/2 cup finely chopped dill

1 teaspoon salt

2/3 teaspoon pepper

3 teaspoons sugar

Beat egg yolks with oil; add vinegar, a few drops at a time, beating steadily. Beat in mustards and dill, then salt, pepper and sugar. Mix well and chill. 8 or more servings.

ROCK CORNISH HENS

4 Cornish hens
Salt
Pepper
Melted butter
1/2 cup beef broth

Preheat oven at 350° Salt and pepper hens. Brush hens with butter. Place hens breast side up in pan and bake for 1/2 hour. Pour beef broth over hens and baste. Bake another 45 minutes, basting every 15 minutes. 4-6 servings.

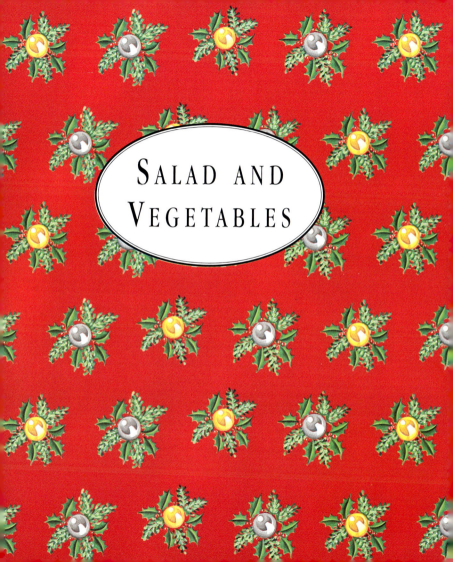

SALAD AND VEGETABLES

CRANBERRY PINEAPPLE MOLD WITH CREAM TOPPING

TOPPING:

> 1/2 pint light cream
> 1/2 cup sugar
> 1/2 cup water
> 1/2 pint sour cream
> 1 package unflavored gelatin
> 2 tablespoons hot water
> 1 teaspoon vanilla

Add sugar to light cream and boil. Mix gelatin and 2 tablespoons hot water; let stand and add to cream when cooled. Add sour cream, 1/2 cup water, and vanilla to topping mixture. Pour into mold and refrigerate for 3 hours.

MOLD:

> 2 packages raspberry flavored gelatin
> 1-1/2 cups hot water

1 large can crushed pineapple (with juice)
2 large cans whole berry cranberry sauce

After topping has jelled, mix fruit ingredients and pour into mold. Refrigerate until set. Unmold and serve. 8 servings.

Sweet Potato Pudding

2 cups cooked sweet potatoes

1 cup hot milk

1/2 teaspoon salt

2 tablespoons sugar

2 tablespoons butter

2 eggs, separated

1 tablespoon nutmeg

1 cup broken nut meats (optional)

Mash sweet potatoes thoroughly. Scald milk. Heat salt, sugar, and butter in milk, stirring until butter is melted. Add this mixture to potatoes. Mix and beat until smooth. Beat egg yolks well and add to potatoes. Add nutmeg. Beat egg whites until stiff; fold into potatoes and pour mixture into buttered baking dish. Bake in 350° oven until brown. Serve at once. 6 servings.

CANDIED SWEET POTATOES

6 sweet potatoes
3/4 cup brown sugar
3/4 cup butter
1/2 cup hot water

Cook sweet potatoes in boiling water to cover until nearly tender. Drain potatoes, peel, slice lengthwise, and place in buttered baking dish. Make syrup of brown sugar, butter, and water. Pour over potatoes and bake at 375° for 25 minutes. 6-8 servings.

STUFFED ZUCCHINI SQUASH

8 medium zucchini

4 cups soft bread crumbs

1 cup grated cheese, divided

1 medium onion, minced

3 tablespoons minced parsley

1 teaspoon salt

1/8 teaspoon pepper

2 eggs, beaten

3 tablespoons butter

Trim ends of zucchini and cut in half lengthwise. Remove pulp with spoon and combine with bread crumbs, 3/4 cup grated cheese, onion, parsley, salt, pepper, and eggs. Fill zucchini shells with mixture and put in baking dish. Dot with butter and sprinkle with remaining cheese. Bake in 350° oven 1/2 hour. 8 servings.

POTATO PUFFS

2 cups cold mashed potatoes
2 tablespoons flour
Salt and pepper to taste
1 egg
1 teaspoon baking powder
Fat for frying

Blend well together in mixer. Drop a teaspoonful at a time in hot fat. Fry slowly until the puffs become brown. When well puffed, drain on brown paper.

BAKED EGGPLANT IN THE SHELL

1 medium eggplant
2 tablespoons butter
1 small onion, grated
1/4 cup bread crumbs
1 egg yolk
1/4 pound American cheese, grated
Salt and pepper to taste

Parboil eggplant until tender, but not soft. Cut in half crosswise. Scrape out seeds and discard them. Scrape out meat and mash with butter, onion, bread crumbs, egg yolk, cheese, and salt and pepper to taste. Refill shell halves and dot with butter. Bake in 350° oven for approximately 20 minutes or until heated through.

GLAZED ONIONS

18 small white onions
1 tablespoon butter
2 tablespoons sugar

Wash and peel onions; cook in water to cover until tender; drain. Melt butter and sugar; add onions and cook over low heat until golden brown, turning occasionally. 6 servings.

MINT-GLAZED CARROTS
WITH PEAS

3 medium carrots, cut in strips
2 cups fresh peas
4 tablespoons butter, divided
Salt and pepper to taste
4 tablespoons sugar
1/2 tablespoon chopped mint leaves

Cook carrots in boiling, salted water 15 minutes; drain.
Cook peas in boiling, salted water about 8 to 10 minutes;
drain and season with 2 tablespoons butter, salt, and
pepper. Glaze carrot strips in mixture of sugar, remaining
2 tablespoons butter, and mint leaves. Place peas in
serving dish and add carrots.

SQUASH AU GRATIN

5 small summer squash
4 tablespoons butter
Salt and pepper to taste
2 eggs
Bread crumbs
1/4 pound Cheddar cheese

Cut and boil squash until tender. Drain and put through colander. Add butter, salt and pepper, and well beaten egg. Pour into buttered baking dish; cover with bread crumbs and grated cheese. Bake at 350° about 30 minutes.

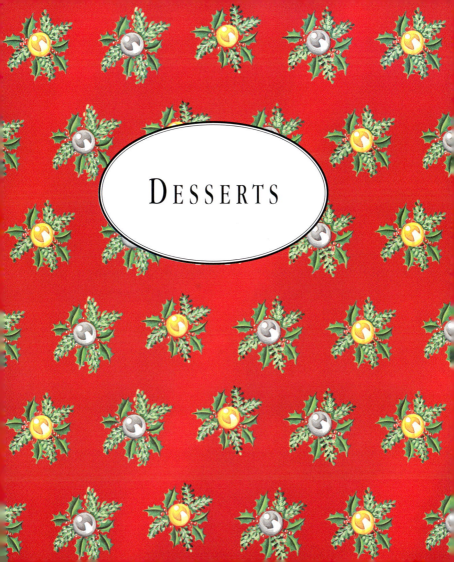

DESSERTS

SOUTHERN PECAN PIE

1 cup sugar
1/2 cup corn syrup
1/4 cup butter, melted
3 eggs, well beaten
1 cup pecans, broken
1 unbaked pie shell

Mix sugar, syrup and butter; add eggs and pecans. Fill unbaked pie shell with mixture and bake for 10 minutes at 400°, then for 30 to 35 minutes at 350°. Serve either cold or hot. Delicious topped with whipped cream.

DANISH APPLE CAKE

1 package zwieback
1 cup sugar
1/2 cup butter
8 tart apples, pared, cored, and sliced
1/2 cup heavy cream, whipped

Crush or grind zwieback and mix with sugar. Brown butter slowly in heavy frying pan. Do not burn. Stir into crumb mixture. Cover bottom of greased casserole with layer of crumbs; cover with sliced apples. Repeat layers of crumbs and apples until all are used, finishing with layer of crumbs on top. Bake in 325° oven for 1-1/4 hours, or until crusty. Serve with cream. 8 servings.

SWEDISH PANCAKES

3 eggs, separated
2 tablespoons sugar
1/8 teaspoon salt
3 tablespoons butter, melted
1/2 cup sifted flour
1-1/2 cups milk
Lingonberry preserves
Powdered sugar

Beat egg yolks with sugar, salt, and melted butter. Stir in flour and milk alternately and mix well. Let stand in a cool place until ready to use. Then whip egg whites until stiff and mix into batter.

Grease heated Swedish pancake pan or ordinary skillet with melted butter and pour or spoon a little batter for each pancake. Pancake browns almost at once. Turn pancake and let other side brown. Transfer cakes to warmed plates, arranging them 5 or 6 on a plate, in circle; spoon lingonberry preserves in middle. Sprinkle cakes with powdered sugar and serve. 2 dozen or more cakes.

APPLE PIE

3 pounds tart green apples
1 cup sugar
2 tablespoons flour
1/8 teaspoon salt
1 teaspoon cinnamon
1/4 teaspoon nutmeg
Pastry for 9-inch double-crust pie
4 tablespoons butter

Peel apples and slice thin. Add sugar mixed with flour, salt, and spices. Fill pastry-lined pie pan. Dot with butter. Adjust top crust. Bake at 450° for 10 minutes, then at 350° for about 40 minutes. 6 servings.

PUMPKIN PIE

1-1/4 cups strained, cooked pumpkin

2/3 cup sugar

1/2 teaspoon salt

2/3 teaspoon ginger

1 teaspoon cinnamon

1/4 teaspoon nutmeg

3 eggs, separated

1-1/4 cups scalded milk

1 6-ounce can (3/4 cup) evaporated milk

1 unbaked 9-inch pie shell

Thoroughly mix pumpkin, sugar, salt, and spices. Add egg yolks and milk, and blend. Fold in beaten egg whites. Pour into 9-inch pastry-lined pie pan. Bake at 450° for 10 minutes, then at 325° for about 45 minutes, or until mixture does not stick to knife. Top with whipped cream, if desired. 6 servings.

EGG NOG PIE

3 egg yolks
1/2 cup sugar
2 cups light cream
1/8 teaspoon salt
1/8 teaspoon nutmeg
Rum to taste
3 stiff-beaten egg whites
1 unbaked 9-inch pie shell

Beat egg yolks, sugar, and cream. Add salt, nutmeg, and rum. Fold in egg whites. Pour into 9-inch pastry-lined pie pan. Bake in 450° oven 10 minutes, then in 325° oven until firm, about 25 minutes. For a very rich dessert, top with slightly sweetened whipped cream. Garnish pie with red and green candy flowers, made from candied rinds.

FRESH COCONUT PIE

2 cups coconut, freshly grated, divided
2 cups milk
1/4 cup coconut milk
1/2 cup sugar
5 tablespoons flour
2 tablespoons cornstarch
1/4 teaspoon salt
3 beaten egg yolks
1/2 teaspoon vanilla
1/2 teaspoon lemon extract
1 drop almond extract
1 baked pie shell
1/2 pint cream, whipped

Scald 1 cup of coconut with milk and coconut milk in double boiler about 20 minutes; strain. Discard solids. Return liquid to double boiler. Mix sugar, flour, cornstarch, and salt; add all at once to hot liquid and cook, stirring constantly, until thickened. Cover and let cook 15 minutes. Stir in egg yolks and cook a minute longer. Remove from heat, add flavorings and most of remaining coconut, and let cool thoroughly before spreading in pie shell. Shortly before serving, cover with whipped cream and sprinkle remaining coconut on top. 6 servings.

CHRISTMAS LOG

5 large eggs, separated
2/3 cup sugar
6 oz. semi-sweet chocolate
3 tablespoons strong coffee
Cocoa
1-1/4 cups heavy cream, whipped

Butter a 12" x 8" baking sheet. Line it with waxed paper and butter paper. Beat egg yolks and sugar with a rotary beater or electric mixer until thick and pale in color. Combine chocolate and coffee and place over low heat. Stir until chocolate melts. Let mixture cool slightly, then stir it into egg yolks. Beat egg whites until stiff and fold them in. Spread mixture evenly on prepared baking sheet and bake 15 minutes at 350°, or until a knife inserted in the middle comes out clean. Do not overbake.

Remove pan from oven and cover cake with a damp cloth. Let stand 30 minutes or until cool. Loosen cake from baking sheet and dust cake generously with cocoa. Turn cake out on waxed paper, cocoa side down, and carefully remove paper from bottom of cake. Spread cake with whipped cream, sweetened and flavored to taste, and roll up like a jelly roll. For easy rolling, firmly grasp each corner of waxed paper on which cake was turned out and flip over about two inches of the edge on top of cake. Continue to roll by further lifting waxed paper. The last roll should deposit the log on a long platter. Cover top with whipped cream. Garnish with chocolate shavings and holly sprigs. 8 servings.

FLAN

6 egg yolks
1/4 cup sugar
1 cup milk
1 cup light cream
3/4 teaspoon vanilla
1/8 teaspoon salt

Beat egg yolks; stir in rest of ingredients. Put 6 custard cups in baking dish, sides of which are higher than cups, then pour boiling water into dish to a level of 1 inch. Pour custard mixture into cups, and bake at 350° for about 30 minutes, or until knife inserted into custard comes out clean. Serve either hot or cold.